KW-220-732

GREAT PR

BULLET GUIDE

Contents

About the author

Brian Salter began his career in the BBC, where he produced and presented features, business and current affairs programmes.

He left the BBC to join Heathrow Airport as Media Relations Manager immediately following the bombing of PanAm 103 over Lockerbie, and was responsible for improving relations with the resident press and for crisis communications at the airport.

From there he moved to a variety of communication roles, but by the 1990s he had started his own consultancy, advising companies and giving training on PR, marketing and presentation techniques, as well as internet technology for business use, when it was still in its infancy.

In 1999 he moved to the Middle East, working in Saudi Arabia, Abu Dhabi and Dubai, where he continues to write for a number of media outlets across the world and gives training on a wide variety of business-related activities.

Introduction

Public relations is primarily human relations – the psychology of interrelating with different audiences – and a critical aspect of growing a business. Everything you say and do is part of your PR campaign. It's the image you project to everyone you meet. It's about your company becoming a force in the public eye on a regular basis.

This book looks at the different elements of public relations, and at the media revolution that is changing the way we do PR. However, the internet could be said to be bringing public relations back to its roots. What is PR after all but the intention to **communicate**, build **relationships** and **influence** people? The new media channels allow us to do all this with a mass audience as never before.

This change of culture requires nothing less than a completely new approach to PR. This book takes a step back from the old ways of tackling PR, and offers a roadmap for using the new PR tools for maximum impact. It will show you how to take advantage of all that PR can offer your company or clients.

1 Who needs PR?

Sending the right message

Public relations is the practice of conveying messages to the public with the intention of changing their actions by **influencing** their opinions. People who work in PR are skilled publicists who present a company or individual to the world in the best light; and PR is used to build rapport with employees, customers, investors, voters or the general public.

PR aims to change the public's actions by influencing their opinions

· ·

> **'Public relations is about reputation – the result of what you do, what you say and what others say about you.'**
>
> Chartered Institute of Public Relations (CIPR)

Companies that want to be regarded in a better light are turning increasingly to **building links** with their various target groups.

Online PR follows the same principles as traditional public relations but offers even more benefits:

* Traditional PR is merely a **one-way conversation**.
* Online PR provides an **interactive conversation**, allowing firms to communicate directly with their target audiences.

PR and driving cultural change

Significantly, many in-house communications departments are being asked to drive through significant **internal cultural change** programmes, in collaboration with their human resources department.

Internal communications is regarded as a major PR discipline for the future, as employees become significant stakeholders in their own right and act as **'brand champions'**.

Before they can do this, they first have to understand their company's core values and ensure that they accord with their own personal values.

Corporate Social Responsibility (CSR) policies are also seen as critical to the long-term success of a company – being recognized as making a real contribution in each society in which it operates.

CSR policies include the public interest in corporate decision making, so that company activities have a positive impact on the wider community and the environment.

4

The art of relating to your particular public – small or global – is a **social skill** we all must develop to some degree, or suffer the loss.

How many worthwhile causes have failed because they were not able to get their message across to those that mattered? Understanding what PR can achieve is an essential component of success.

PR is primarily the **psychology of interrelationships.**

* Everything you say and do is part of your PR campaign.
* It is the image you project every day to everyone you meet.
* It is about you and your company becoming a force in the public eye on a regular basis.

'The public is the only critic whose opinion is worth anything at all.'
Mark Twain

Perception is everything

PR practitioners **work with facts, perception and truth** every day. It's what we do for a living. As practitioners, we talk almost casually about changing perceptions – but what does that really mean?

Perception is the process by which humans collect information and a basis for how humans see things. When we talk about changing perceptions, we mean two things:

1 changing individuals' ways of **perceiving**
2 changing their **understanding** and opinions.

So, PR has two functions: education and persuasion.

* **Education** seeks to change the way someone perceives an event.
* **Persuasion** seeks to change how the individual interprets facts that have been perceived.

6

Understanding and opinion

This brings us to a distinction that is too often ignored.

* **Knowledge** leads to understanding.
* Opinion is **judgement**, or a formed conclusion.

There are two basic states of understanding:

1 good   2 poor.

However, we can identify three possible types of opinion:

1 good   2 bad   3 neutral.

* If the individual is on our side and knows us well, we reinforce his or her understanding and opinion.
* If the individual knows us well and can't stand us, we try to rebut the person's negative comments.
* If the individual doesn't know us well, but thinks highly of us, we educate that person about us and reinforce the good opinion.

Communication

Without exception, communication lies at the heart of every successful – and unsuccessful – business

It's obvious that any business needs to communicate with everyone who has anything to do with it.

* What…?
* How…?
* Why…?

* When…?
* With whom…?
* Where…?

are the **key questions** to be asked with every form of communication.

Sometimes, what organizations wish to say to one audience will **not necessarily be the same** as what they wish to say to another. Likewise, the feedback they solicit from one audience may not be what they solicit or receive from another.

Getting to know your audience

Knowing your audience is crucial. Before developing a PR campaign, you need to research your audience and what it wants. Your strategy needs to be tailored to the audience, and not just about the organization you are representing. External audiences, for instance, may be given a slightly glossier picture of the fortunes of a company than those within the organization.

There will almost certainly be those, too, who will need to be 'in the know' with regard to any bad news or commercially sensitive information; and so **getting to know your audiences** has to be a **key consideration** in any PR campaign.

Remember
There is a very fine dividing line between showing something in a good light and giving misleading information.

Knowing what to communicate

Just as important as identifying the key audiences with whom you wish to communicate is **knowing what it is you want to communicate**, and why you are trying to say it in the first place.

Surely that's obvious isn't it?

Actually, it isn't!

It is surprising how many organizations 'open their mouths before putting their brains into gear'.

Communications can only really be viewed in a **holistic way**; otherwise one could argue that the whole exercise is a waste of time.

Knowing what it is you want to communicate is only half the story. Nowadays, there is a **veritable plethora of communication channels** available, some of which are good in some situations, but hopeless in others.

Social media releases
Competitions
Webcasts
Press release distribution
Photography
Online surveys
Online media centres
TV interviews
Skypecasts
Press releases
Tagged photography
Online media relations
VNR
Webchats
Media relations
Stunts
Press trips
Radio interviews
Investor relations
Advertorials
Podcasts/vodcasts
Internet radio
Audio features
Surveys
Stunts
Viral
Virtual world events
RSS feeds
Infographics
Guerrilla activity
White papers
Folksonomies
APIs
Blogger relations
Newsletters
Microblogs
Social network
Search engine optimised
Internal communications
Reputation
Management
Brand publications
Internal blogs
WIKIs
Corporate/brand blogs
Interviews
Brand activity
Conferences
Stakeholder relations
Forums/boards/comments
Crisis management
Social search
Stakeholder mapping
Social bookmarking
Press briefings
Social networking events
P2P
Events
Search Engine optimised releases
Crowdsourcing
Social networking
Online monitoring
Product launches
Online surveytorials

And as more and more people ditch printed media to seek their news online, traditional PR agencies as well as newspapers will have to adjust to survive and keep up.

2 More effective communication

What is communication?

Communication is a word that can mean everything and nothing at the same time. All businesses need to communicate with:

* their **employees**, if they want the best out of them
* **suppliers**, if they want the right raw materials at the best price
* **shareholders**, if they want to keep them on side
* **customers**, if they want to make a profit
* the **community** at large, since no one can work in isolation.

Successful communication applies as much to manufacturing industries as it does to service sector or public sector organizations; but **few people are taught to communicate** in a manner suitable for business.

In social communication we can afford to be sloppy in what we say, since in general both parties know one another and can take it that things left unsaid can be taken as understood. In a business environment, however, communication has to be:

* clear   * precise   * unambiguous.

If you want to avoid misunderstandings at some later date, it also needs to be:

* **formal** in nature   * **planned** carefully.

Communication is a word that can mean everything and nothing at the same time

Communication: a two-way process

> Communication requires a minimum of two parties.

Although one party may be the initial sender of a message and the other the receiver, both sides need to take on both roles if successful communication is to occur.

Ideas communicated can be:

* **verbal**, in the sense of spoken, written or emailed words, for instance
* **graphical**, encompassing any message that can be encapsulated as a visual image.

After all, we all know that a picture can paint a thousand words.

Although these **direct channels** are essential elements of communication, there are a number of other **indirect channels** that many businesses ignore, but which can be a major source of poor communication if handled improperly. These indirect channels include:

* body language
* context and environment
* cultural signals.

Think of the importance of body language, for instance. **We are all very quick to make instant judgements** about people by the way they look or the body signals they give off. In a similar way, the online presence of a company says a lot about the organization itself, and this can **reinforce** or even **negate** previous opinions held about that establishment.

'There is only one thing in the world worse than being talked about, and that is not being talked about.'

Oscar Wilde

Web 2.0 and social media

Content is the new democracy, and the people are ensuring that their voices are heard. The advent of 'Web 2.0' in 2004 has created a new layer of influencers. **'Ordinary' people** not only read and disseminate information, but also interactively **share and create content for others**.

Using social media, people now have the ability to impact and influence the decisions of their peers and also other newsmakers. Social media is not a game you can view from the sidelines.

* Those who participate will succeed.
* Everyone else will either have to catch up or miss out altogether.
* Just sending out messages is no longer an option.

Content is the new democracy

As American IT journalist David 'Doc' Searls once wrote:

'There is no market for messages.'

Whether you use the internet or more traditional tools for your PR, if your customers don't trust you as a company because of something they may have heard about you, then it **may not matter what you say to them** because everything you do say will be **treated with cynicism** or simply not believed.

Even internally, people may communicate well within their own department, but **may not see the overall picture** of what their company is trying to achieve. This is because they are blinded by the need to fulfil their department's objectives at the expense of other departments, which **they may see as competitors**.

PR in the workplace

It's unfortunate that in many businesses a large proportion of employees:

1   have **little or no contact** with the
    company's customers
2   are **blind to the problems experienced**
    by the very people who pay their
    wages – those selfsame customers.

Higher up in the organization, some
executives **communicate their
decisions** down the corporate ladder
with little comprehension of what
impact those decisions will have, either
on the company or on the people who
have to implement them.

Likewise, some managers lack enthusiasm for change. They may even feel stressed in implementing the executives' wishes. The result is that the rest of the workforce:

* feel unappreciated
* have no clear focus
* feel in the dark as to the overall picture in which they play such an important role.

Good PR is all about **two-way conversations**. And the new social media is all about speaking *with*, not 'to' or 'at', people. As the old saying goes, the best communicators start as the best listeners.

'Markets are conversatio

David 'Doc' Se

Language: the core of communications

Ever since man set foot on this earth, language has been at the heart of communication. We all think we are terribly good at it. Unfortunately, the reality is very different.

Think of an email, where someone has responded to you with a simple 'OK' to a statement you made. It's unclear whether he means:

> OK. I'll think about it.

or

> OK. I agree with you.

Depending on what you take the response to mean, your subsequent actions could be totally different, which could lead to totally different outcomes. Such **misunderstandings** are common in email correspondence, when we often click Send before thinking about how the recipient will perceive our message.

As we have seen, language is at the core of all communications. And the way we use language can make the difference between effective and ineffective communications. Now that the internet is breaking down communication barriers between countries, there is one overarching golden rule: **keep it simple.**

Remember

With any use of language keep it simple:

* Stick to the facts, don't over-complicate and don't use jargon.
* Cut out unnecessary words: using fewer words means that every word has more impact.
* Customize copy for different audiences, and don't forget to proofread everything.

When PR is done well it looks easy, but it isn't. Usually, if you have done it well it's **because you have done it simply.**

3 Why is digital PR important?

Online PR: a revolution

These are exciting times for public relations professionals. With the advent of the internet, what is happening now has never happened before; and online PR is completely changing the way we communicate with our audiences.

Social media and user-generated content are creating **new opportunities** for planning PR strategies and increasing a brand's visibility. What is happening to PR now is nothing short of a revolution.

What is happening to PR now is nothing short of a revolution

It is estimated that approximately **1.67 billion people** worldwide use the internet, a figure that has risen by well over **1,000 per cent** in the past eight years. In short, online users are ensuring that the word 'public' is being put back into 'public relations'.

The new ways of doing PR have been given a variety of names...

* digital PR
* online PR
* PR 2.0
* online communications
* social media PR
* digital communications

...but they all amount to the same thing. **Digital PR** appears (at the moment) to be the most generally accepted term.

The world of Web 2.0

Most internet users speak English. Although the total number of native English speakers in the world is about **325 million**, over **1.2 billion** people speak English as a second language. Around **45 per cent of all web pages** are written in English.

The metamorphosis of the internet into 'Web 2.0' changed everything for the PR community.

Web 2.0 is commonly associated with web pages that **facilitate interactive information sharing**. Such sites allow users to collaborate with one another in a social media setting as **creators of user-generated content in a virtual community**. This contrasts with websites that limit users to the passive viewing of content created for them.

Examples of Web 2.0 include:

* social-networking sites	* hosted services
* blogs	* web applications
* wikis	* mashups
* video-sharing sites	* folksonomies.

'Technology is shifting power away from editors, the publishers, the establishment, the media elite. Now it's the people who are taking control.'

Rupert Murdoch, to *Wired* magazine, 2006

World Wide Web inventor Tim Berners-Lee has challenged the idea that Web 2.0 is qualitatively different from previous web technologies, saying that the web was always meant to be 'people to people'.

Social media: the heart of the new PR

If you think about it, **social media** – defined by Wikipedia as '…an umbrella term that defines the various activities that integrate technology, social interaction, and the construction of words and pictures' – **is at the very heart of what PR is all about**. The idea of the Web, as dreamed up by its inventor, Sir Tim Berners-Lee, was that it should be 'a collaborative space where people can interact'.

Since the internet – especially the coming of Web 2.0 – has brought about a change in tools, a change in platform and a change in the culture of public relations, PR requires a completely new approach.

'The Web as I envisaged it, we have not seen it yet. The future is still so much bigger than the past.'

Tim Berners-Lee

30

And yet, what has changed?

> It's still about
> building relationships and
> influencing people!

It could be argued that it is exactly the same – **building relationships in order to influence people** – and that digital PR is a purer form of what PR used to be, but which somehow got diverted along the way, growing into various other areas. So all that digital PR is doing is putting things back where they should be.

New opportunities

Digital PR offers huge new opportunities – but how do you sort out the professionals from the amateurs? Part of the problem now is that older PR establishments are way behind the mainstream players where digital PR is concerned.

* More than half of online PR is now done by **non-PR-trained** professionals.
* Nearly half of all **clients are dissatisfied** with their agency's online PR offerings.
* There is relatively **little training** and support from industry representative bodies.
* Other digital marketing disciplines are filling the digital PR chasm.

No longer can you rely on your press releases or website to deliver your PR messages: **the world is overwhelmed with information.** You're better off reaching audiences where they are most likely to respond (for example in social networks), or where they will be looking for *your* information when the timing is right for them.

Experiment with different platforms to learn new ways in which you can:

1 **LISTEN** to your publics
2 **IDENTIFY** influencers
3 **ENGAGE** with multiple stakeholders
4 **MEASURE** outputs.

But the **more you learn**, the more you'll soon realize **you don't know**!

More and more companies are finding that by embracing networks they can control, such as Twitter, Facebook and YouTube, as well as blog-powered websites, they can truly connect with their audience and build brand loyalty.

A shift in emphasis

What we need is nothing short of a total shift in emphasis from traditional to digital PR:

Traditional PR	Digital PR
✳ Core contacts and networks	✳ Larger networks changing rapidly
✳ Catch-all media materials	✳ Tailored materials
✳ Structured	✳ Conversational
✳ Pagination restrictions	✳ No pagination
✳ Key influencers = journalists, analysts, etc.	✳ Key influencers = are who??
✳ Return on investment difficult to measure	✳ ROI easier to measure

There are now plenty of online forums, which provide a really **good opportunity** from a brand point of view to listen to **what people have to say** about your brand or product.

Individuals have gained a disproportionate level of influence. A blogger in his bedroom, for instance, can reach a global readership – and this totally changes the balance. This means that **older PR models need to adapt.**

Problem	Solution
* Sheer volume of online information	* Tools to help filter what's useful
* Wider range of media	* New coverage or monitoring models
* Influencers changing	* More effective messaging required
* The speed that messages spread through networks	* Crisis teams and procedures must adapt
* Brand/corporate attack	* Early warning systems and use of Web 2.0 technology and tools

The move from traditional to digital PR is nothing short of a paradigm shift

4 Understanding your audiences

Tailoring your message

When planning a PR strategy, you have to **identify all your audiences** before you can even begin to work on the detail of what you wish to get across to them. You need to work out, in simple terms, answers to the following questions:

* **What** am I trying to say?
* **Why** do I want to say it?
* To **whom** am I saying it?
* **How** do I intend to say it?

Not all audiences will require the same information, or even require it in the same format. Many people are so anxious to get talking that they **don't stop to think** what it is the potential recipient **might want to know**.

Not all audiences require the same information in the same format

If you draw up a list of recipients and then highlight the relationship between the various groups, **the relationship between the messages then becomes much clearer**.

Business success depends upon customers; and since the advent of the internet, **never have real customer communications been more important**. Knowing your customers and keeping them happy is therefore at the heart of an effective PR strategy.

Keeping the customer happy

Over the past 30 years everything has been turned on its head. Until the 1950s, most people were satisfied with products that worked; choice wasn't an issue and purchasing was done on the basis of need rather than want. Since then, increasing competition and a rise in customer expectations mean that today's company **must communicate brilliantly** with its customers, or it will simply die.

The main reasons why customers become one-off and **do not come back for more**, rather than just on price alone, are:

1 poor service
2 a lack of understanding of their needs
3 arrogance on the part of the organization.

Why should a prospective customer bother with you if your competitors are only too happy to communicate with them and you're not?

CASE STUDY: British Caledonian

In the 1970s, the now-defunct independent airline British Caledonian, which flew to a number of destinations in the Middle East, Europe and South America, had as its slogan: 'We never forget you have a choice.'

They listened to what their customers said about them.

They were competing against the big national carriers and knew that **they could only compete on the level of service** they offered. BCal's service was second to none, and this was amply demonstrated by their repeat passenger figures. (The company was eventually taken over by the much larger British Airways.)

Over the past 30 years everything has been turned on its head

Gathering feedback

Measuring opinion is a **crucial part** of building a successful public relations plan. A company that gets **genuine feedback** from its customers and target groups will be **better equipped** to know how to impart the very messages that it wants to get across.

In the past, consumer surveys and questionnaires were widely used to:

* garner the views of prospective customers
* identify trends for more in-depth and specific research.

Now, social media and Web 2.0 take this feedback gathering to a whole new level, undreamed of just a decade or two back.

42

'Public opinion is the thermometer a monarch should constantly consult.'
Napoleon Bonaparte

Meeting customer expectations

* Customers want what they have been promised… and more… and will always hold the company responsible for non-delivery.
* Customers now have the means to **tell the whole world** about your non-delivery.
* **Most customers only want to get good service** and be told the truth about delivery, quality, terms and conditions.
* No longer can you fall back on the legal small print. It may be legally right, but is it **losing you sales because of its attitude**?

Seeing other points of view

The majority of businesses get their raw materials from an outside **supplier**. Although traditional communications have been based on beating them down to the lowest possible price, **this does not make for good long-term business relationships**.

* Put yourself in the shoes of your suppliers and things begin to look a bit different.
* **Check your corporate mindset** toward suppliers and **amend your attitude** if it is not going to be helpful in times of need.
* Try to see any problems from **their** point of view, and communicate that you have understood them.

'There is nothing insignificant in the world. It all depends on the point of view.'
Johann Wolfgang von Goethe

Regardless of how well a business is doing, it must constantly keep its **owners and shareholders** well informed about the **current state of the organization**.

Owners invariably start many of the communication processes by **asking endless questions of the board** to which they want answers.

Shareholders tend to be either:

1 institutional	2 private

and both types need to be kept informed.

It is also necessary to communicate effectively with:

✳ brokers	✳ analysts	✳ the financial press

This is especially – but not necessarily only – true for larger companies.

'Ordinary' shareholders tend to be influenced by the financial press, and so **your communications strategy ignores them at their peril**.

Complying with regulations

We work in a world dominated by **regulations**, usually set by some governmental or professional body. Many impose **considerable costs** on a business but **every business needs to comply with them**.

* Larger companies can employ **lobbyists** on their behalf, both to monitor and to put forward their views about regulations that affect them to the bureaucrats.

* Smaller businesses can use their **collective membership** of bodies – such as Chambers of Commerce and professional institutes – to represent them.

Community relations

Many larger firms **actively encourage involvement in the community** in some way, effectively making a bridge between themselves and the local community, and **improving the perception of themselves** in the process.

The **perceptions of people** in the vicinity of your business can have **an important impact** on local regulations or on your attempts to recruit the right staff.

However, there are several things you should do before embarking on a Community Relations programme:

* **Calculate** how much time as well as money you want to devote to it.
* **Be realistic** and try to choose a programme that has **good photo opportunities**.
* Make sure **you tell the world** at large about it – locally, regionally and nationally!

5 Dealing with the media

Media relations

Good media relations can be critical for any business, and play a significant role in the fortunes of a company. Businesses should understand the importance of good relationships with journalists, who can be an effective mouthpiece for you. It's therefore in every company's interest to nurture them.

* From a journalist's perspective, companies are often **too confidential** about their businesses.
* From an organization's perspective, journalists can sometimes be too nosy.

Good media relations can be critical for any business

It's important to understand that journalists have a job to do:

* broadcasters need to **fill air time**
* print journalists need to **fill column inches**
* new media journalists need to **fill web pages**.

When you give journalists a good story, you are **doing them a favour**. Journalists need good stories, so don't waste their time giving them stories that are substandard or irrelevant.

It is the PR person's role to put the jargon of their company's trade into plain, simple language and to present it to journalists **in a form they can use**.

Newsroom journalists

A newsroom, whether print or electronic, is an **information factory** producing and packaging **editorial content** for consumers. Newsroom journalists are **gatekeepers and filters of information** at both fact gathering and editing levels. A typical newsroom is buried in information, but it might not be the right, complete or appropriate information for the specific outlet.

Journalists are bound by a number of different factors:

* **assignments** handed to them by editors
* their **personal attitudes** and bias
* their **education** and understanding
* **editorial** stance
* their **commitment** to the story
* the ability to **express themselves**
* **word count** or **airtime deadlines**.

If a company's facts are not compelling, its stories are **lost in the information flow**. It must always compete for coverage: *If it gets into the news, someone else doesn't.*

52

If organizations have compelling news, it may be published, whether or not they wish to communicate it.

A PR practitioner must strategize how best to:

1 present the story to **gain a positive result**, if the news is good
2 **mitigate negatives**, if the news is bad.

The practitioner:

* gathers facts
* sets up interviews
* provides graphics and visuals
* gains access for reporters to key people
* assists the reporter before and after news is published.

'Journalism is the ability to meet the challenge of filling space.'

Rebecca West

The PR practitioner as intermediary

PR practitioners are intermediaries who try to satisfy both sides, although this is not always possible. Reporters appreciate knowledgeable practitioners who steer them in the right direction and save the journalist time in reporting a story. A PR practitioner's credibility with a reporter comes through transactional experience, through contact, whether direct or indirect:

* **delivering information** and interviews the reporter needs
* **counselling his superiors** and company directors on when to deal with reporters, and how
* providing **clear and accurate facts** to the reporter, whether good or bad
* **being there** when a reporter calls, and handling a reporter's request quickly and accurately.

PR practitioners are intermediaries who try to satisfy both sides

Three key points for PR people

1 A reporter gains credibility by reporting fairly and accurately. If you find a reporter inaccurate, go elsewhere to get your message out.

2 Because a reporter may deal with a PR practitioner once or infrequently, it is up to the practitioner to know and become well known to reporters and not vice versa.

3 Practitioners who make no attempt to **cultivate reporters** consign themselves to low credibility with news media and to lack of access when they need it.

Cultivating reporters

Reporters reach large numbers of individuals and directly influence opinions about:

* reputations
* products
* services
* issues
* individuals.

That's why reporters are so important, and **why they are worth cultivating**. Developing and maintaining good relationships with reporters is one of the key tasks of the PR practitioner.

56

However, as in the whole of life, **we all perceive the world from our own perspective**, and journalists are no different. The best situation is a **reporter with an open mind** and without a conclusion. It is possible to educate the reporter in this case.

Remember
* **Maintaining a spirit of accuracy** is the best way to build credibility with reporters who value accuracy.
* **Maintaining a spirit of service** towards reporters and their needs enhances a practitioner's credibility because a reporter has to get a job done.
* **Working with a deadline mentality** supports reporters who live by deadlines.
* **Arrogance doesn't become PR practitioners** who value truth, facts and correct perception. They understand how difficult it is to get things right.

Ways to get media coverage

Despite all the counselling, strategy, partnerships, writing and more, **CEOs want media coverage.**

Until the industry creates better measurement systems, **a full-page story** in a broadsheet newspaper becomes a tangible 'product' that you can hold in your hands and **show to your boss**!

This is despite the fact that **internet coverage can often reach thousands more** end-users and have a **considerably bigger impact** than hard-copy print or broadcasts.

Top tips

* Have a good **story**.
* **Know** your media.
* Cultivate **relationships**.
* Create the **unexpected**.
* **Hone your pitch** to a 15-second speech.
* Always ask if a reporter is on **deadline**.
* **Know your story** inside and out.
* Try different **approaches**.
* **Follow up** on potential leads.
* Be **creative**.
* **Good writing** counts.
* Have a **strategy**.

6 Writing powerful press releases

Practical pointers

At least 99 per cent of press releases are **thrown in the bin** – and most of them are written by PR agencies that are charging their clients a fortune. The successful press releases – the ones that lead to a story or interview – have **certain qualities in common**.

As with many things, a few simple rules will guide us through the intricacies of writing a good news release.

One of the primary questions PR practitioners need to ask is *'What is news?'* Journalists stick to a **simple formula**:

Who?	*Where?*	*Why?*
What?	*When?*	*How?*

There's also one more:

Why should anyone care?

Our press release must have news value to the target outlet, contain all the correct information and have a strong angle and focus. The more we strive to hit the right buttons with the media, the better the chances of seeing our story in the press.

News writers and editors take about five to ten seconds to decide whether or not to use your release

Getting creative with press releases

Journalists are not particularly interested in your company, your history or your product or service; which is why press releases with headlines such as:

'Local company celebrates 30 years in business'

or

'XYZ appoints new chairman'

go straight in the bin. **They're boring!** But if the new Chairman of XYZ celebrated his appointment by painting the building pink, that would **gain instant coverage**.

As with most marketing, good news releases are a matter of **being creative** and **thinking** 'outside the box'.

> The best press releases step into the shoes of the journalist or producer reading them, and **meet their needs**.

64

Journalists are under pressure to find stories that are of **interest to their audiences**. If you were reading a publication or listening to a radio show, **what would jump out and appeal to you?** Answer that question and you've got the subject for your press release.

The following are typical items announced via news releases:

* New products
* Improvements to products
* Noteworthy new accounts
* Staff changes
* Quarterly earnings
* Achievements
* Information resources

* Response to a crisis
* Special events
* Charitable donations
* Awards won
* Promotions
* Research findings
* Human-interest stories

'Think like a wise man but communicate in the language of the people.'

W.B. Yeats

What's your objective?

At times, people issue releases without a clear goal or objective in mind. Knowing your objective will give your writing focus and help you select distribution channels. Setting goals will also help you track and measure the overall effectiveness of your strategies.

Knowing your objective gives your writing focus

Below is a mixture of short- and long-term goals:

* Increase or maintain **awareness**
* Establish credibility or **authority**
* **Build client image**
* Get **interviews** on television, radio, internet
* Become an **expert source**
* **Promote** sales

* **Drive traffic** to a special event or website
* Change buyer/industry **behaviour**
* Expand **market share**
* **Comply** with company regulations
* Increase **stock price**

Some people write their news releases with a **short bulleted section** at the front, with the

* Who?
* What?
* When?
* Where?
* How?
* Why?

at the beginning.

After the shorthand section, they then write brief descriptive paragraphs to fill in the details.

Others lead in with a short, pithy opening paragraph.

At the end of the release, you should give accurate contact information – phone numbers, email address, etc.

Remember to date the release and indicate when you want the information released.

Mind your language

One of the most common faults in news release writing is the use of **sloppy language**.

1 As you read through your work, **mentally eliminate words and phrases**. If the piece reads well without the extra language, delete the surplus.
2 If you're writing about one of your many products, **concentrate solely on that product**. It may be tempting to throw in your latest achievement, but if it doesn't support the theme, **resist**!
3 You can always put in extra information in a **'Notes for editors'** section at the end.

> **Strong nouns and verbs** work best. Relying on adjectives and adverbs to put the vigour in your message will result in weaker text.

The headline

The **headline** is the most important part of your press release. If it doesn't grab the journalists' attention, your press release is heading for the dustbin.

The headline needs to be **bold and interesting**. It needs to **stand out** from all the other press releases.

If you were selling a new supplement to help indigestion, which of these two press releases do you think would get the best response?

New Supplement helps Ease Indigestion
Why Some Foods Explode in Your Stomach

The reason newspapers use bold, **attention-grabbing headlines** is that they work. You can deploy the **same strategy** to grab the attention of the journalists you are trying to reach.

The power of pictures

Adding pictures will give your press release greater impact because:

* a good photo can **move your article** from the back of a magazine **to the front**
* photos can be the **deciding factor** when you're pitching a story idea.

Newspapers typically need a resolution not less than 200dpi (typically generated by a 3 or 4 megapixel camera), while magazines will require much better – 300dpi / 6 megapixel being the minimum acceptable quality.

The photo caption should also explain the '**who**, **where**, **when**, **why**, **how** and **what**' of the picture.

Photos and graphics can be a powerful publicity tool, **helping to sell the story** to the reader – but only if you use them well.

1 Make sure you have good-quality, above-the-shoulders photos of all your **experts** who are likely to be interviewed by the media.
2 Shoot '**environmental portraits**' of your experts working *in situ*. Weekly newspapers that don't have big photo staffs would probably welcome these photos.
3 Make available **interior and exterior shots** of your company.
4 Submit photos with **news releases** about routine announcements.
5 Pie charts and other **graphics** can often help readers understand complicated issues.
6 If you're sponsoring an event, call the picture desk at your local newspaper.

> **'If your pictures aren't good enough, you're not close enough.'**
> Robert Capa

7 The internet's social media

User-generated content and PR

Social media are having a major impact on business communication, and PR practitioners need to know how to harness them to reach customers and build reputation.

Social networking sites such as **Facebook** and **Twitter** are used for connecting friends, relatives and work colleagues. With 500 million people on Facebook and 50 million on Twitter, it's not a question of:

* should we use social media?

but

* are we doing it correctly?

Social media have become appealing for businesses to reach customers and build their reputation

The first step is to tap into online conversations and **listen to your audience**. Social media offer you instant **in-depth research** and **feedback** you've never had access to before. These can all inform your PR strategy and **hone your messaging**.

In the UK and US, social networking accounts for **over 12 per cent** of web traffic – more now than are using search engines such as Google. There are literally hundreds of social media sites, including:

❋ Facebook	❋ Flixster	❋ Digg
❋ YouTube	❋ OleOle	❋ Baby Kingdom
❋ MySpace	❋ StumbleUpon	❋ LiveJournal
❋ Flickr	❋ SlideShare	❋ TripIt
❋ WordPress	❋ Blogger	❋ Goodreads
❋ Last.fm	❋ iLike	❋ SmugMug

Your internet PR plan

Social networks and search engines perform different functions, but **both act as gateways** to the internet. Facebook is the **clear leader** of social networking, accounting for 55 per cent of all visits to social sites, followed by video-sharing site YouTube, with 17 per cent. Facebook can be an **inexpensive** and **very effective tool** if integrated strategically with your internet PR plan.

The following seven steps will help you devise your plan:

1 First you must identify your target audience.
2 Add people you know in the industry.
3 Use groups to find Facebookers with similar interests to your company.
4 Monitor conversations closely to find out what's of interest.
5 Get in touch with the influencers.

6 Then **expand your network** by adding the friends of your friends. Add a creative note in your friend request to get your message through.

7 Always **link to your website**, and do not forget to include your **contact info**.

Facebook alternatives such as MySpace and Bebo receive significantly fewer visits, but **should be included in your PR campaigns**.

Blogs and blogging

The introduction of blog hosting sites such as Live Journal and Blogger propelled the widespread use of blogs. As of January 2009, blog search engine Technorati **recorded over 133 million blogs** indexed back to 2002.

Most blogs are maintained by individuals and are interactive, allowing visitors to leave comments; and **it is this interactivity that distinguishes them** from other, static websites.

Many companies aiming to launch their online PR campaigns have used **livejournal.com**, which is popular among politicians, businessmen and journalists.

The popularity of blogs has also given rise to **'fake blogs'** in which a company will create a fictional blog that appears to come from an unbiased source but which is in fact a marketing tool to promote a product.

78

CASE STUDY: Hennessy Black

By listening online, Hennessy Cognac discovered fans of their brand on BlackPlanet.com, a social networking site for African Americans. Based on this data, Hennessy sponsored African American concerts in major cities across the US, always making content from these events available online.

In 2010 they held a major launch party for their first new product in 50 years: Hennessy Black. The event reached more than 25 million people through a number of websites. Hennessy Black is now mentioned in nearly 1.4 million websites, and Google Images lists over 500,000 references.

Twitter

Twitter is a **microblogging service** that enables users to send and read other users' text-based posts of **up to 140 characters**. With **more than 100 million users** worldwide, Twitter is described as the 'SMS of the internet'.

CASE STUDY: BakerTweet

The Albion Bakery in Shoreditch, London, is using the first BakerTweet device in its café. The baker's followers get a 'tweet' to let them know that something hot and fresh has just come out of the oven and they should get down there pronto.

CASE STUDY: Holiday bookings

The Monarch Hotel in Dubai estimated that Twitter was responsible for about 12 per cent of its Eid holiday bookings in 2010.

Making other links

It's not only journalists and bloggers who can spread your story. It can also be spread by the army of people who use **bookmarking and recommendation sites** such as Digg.com.

Bookmarking is a method for users to organize, store, manage and search for bookmarks of resources online. Unlike file sharing, **the resources themselves aren't shared**, merely bookmarks that reference them.

Get enough links to your stories and you could end up on the front page of Digg and other social media sites. **This can bring a huge number of visitors to your site**.

> **'Twitter lets me hear from a lot of people in a very short period of time.'**
> Robert Scoble

Getting online PR coverage

It really isn't difficult getting online coverage of your company or products. Even small online audiences can be valuable for driving traffic to your site. The following steps will help you get coverage:

1 Make sure **all press releases are visible online** and configured to take advantage of URLs/links, videos, images, sound and other sources of information.
2 **Identify your main keywords** and phrases to be attractive to search engines.
3 Ensure keywords are included in releases **linking to relevant pages** on your site.
4 **Target online editors** and specialist websites.
5 Identify the top 10 bloggers who talk about **subjects relevant to your company**.

Getting online coverage of your company isn't difficult

82

More top tips for great online PR

✳ Online PR requires **social, creative, persuasive and technical skills**.
✳ Develop ongoing **relationships** with editors and bloggers.
✳ Keep an eye on media **industry websites**, such as holdthefrontpage.co.uk.
✳ Keep an eye out for **new services**, applications, tools, etc. Mashable.com is a great site for this.
✳ Enhance your MySpace and Facebook profiles by **updating content** regularly, providing downloads such as web banners and video clips, and creating exclusive online deals.
✳ Provide an online **press centre** to save journalists time and effort, and help you track which publications are using your company's news.

8 Creating more PR opportunities

PR on slow days

What do you do when there is **very little that's newsworthy** around? Does a PR person simply continue to **churn out press releases** about a once hot topic?

The answer is a resounding **NO! Don't waste time** pulling together an expensive press conference about nothing. Instead, **use your time more effectively** and efficiently. **Think more strategically,** and try some of the techniques outlined in this chapter.

Why not prepare a **brief backgrounder** of your company with a list of **'hot topics'** the CEO or a manager could discuss? Journalists are always looking for experts, and invariably they **go for the tried and trusted** every time.

Another useful strategy is to identify a 'hot topic' in the news and **try to find an angle** that your company could get involved in. For example:

* dentists could contact the media during National Smile Week
* accountants could contact the local press before the next budget and tell them they're available for comment on how it will affect local businesses.

With a little lateral thinking you can always find something to say about your company

Boosting your company's profile

There are several tried and tested ways of boosting your company's profile, outlined here.

Write articles

If your people have **expertise** on a specific subject, encourage them to **write an article** about it targeted to their audience.

Perhaps an editor of a trade magazine relevant to your sector would be interested in featuring a **regular column**? They are always on the lookout for well-written articles. Think what a boost this would give your **company's profile** if your clients read about you in such a journal.

88

Attend or host conferences and other events

* Look for upcoming **seminars or conferences** for your company. Draft speaker proposals and submit them to conference organizers that might benefit from your company's expertise. If these are written up in a trade magazine, it will give your company a higher profile.
* Suggest that your company initiates a **round table** providing valuable information to potential and current clients. This should enable you to reap **event publicity**.
* **Host lunches** to introduce specific reporters to your company. Ensure there is someone such as a director who is willing to give **off-the-record briefings** so that the journalist goes away with some **inside information** and feels he or she has benefited from the meeting.

Remember
Planning an event takes time and money, so make sure that you have enough of both for the event you have in mind. You'll also need to be clear about your objectives.

Launch a publicity stunt

Publicity stunts and special events often generate interest and media coverage. Before you rush ahead with a wild idea, though, **think what the stunt will say about your company** or product.

* Will it give you **useful publicity**? If so, go ahead and do it.
* If it's likely to end in controversy, you might wish to rethink your strategy.

CASE STUDY: Barnum's circus elephant

The American showman P.T. Barnum used to announce the arrival of his circus in town by hitching an elephant to a plough beside the train tracks. This raised such a rumpus that it's still reportedly against the law in North Carolina to plough a field with an elephant.

Publicity stunts often generate media coverage

The challenge of any publicity stunt is to **preserve the message** contained within it. How often have you seen a brilliant television commercial, and yet the following day been **hard pressed to say what it was advertising**?

If someone walks a high wire across Niagara Falls wearing the logo of a sponsor, it is **unlikely** the sponsor will **gain much awareness** from it. But promoting a golf club by having a long-ball driving contest **makes a direct connection** between the product offering and promise.

The challenge is to design an event in such a way that the **message is integral rather than buried**.

Do community or charity work

Another easy way to gain quick exposure is to provide a **community or charity service**. Such work is often quite '**promotable**' and allows your company to be known as a **good corporate citizen** among peer companies.

Take advantage of the days when your company doesn't have news to report, and flex your **creative muscle** to **create media opportunities**. For instance, close your business and have everyone do a day of charity work. Headlines would read,

'Local Business Closes Doors to Help the Needy!'

'We make a living by what we get, but we make a life by what we give.'
Winston Churchill

Start a Hall of Fame

Induct some of your industry's top personalities and send out a press release. Each year, induct some more members and send out yet another release!

The media love lists:

1 the best
2 the worst
3 the most
4 the least
5 the top 10
6 the bottom 10.

Lists are perfect for an editor to add a little levity to contrast with harder news.

Add to brand or name recognition with some well-chosen 'prizes'. These would be promotional products adorned with the company logo and the award given.

Craft a cost of living index

A variation on the list concept is to create a **cost of living index**. For instance, 'The Moet Index' is basically a list of the price of a range of luxury items, such as:

* a lobster
* a mink coat
* a jar of caviar
* truffles
* a diamond bracelet
* a bottle of Moet

with the total cost of all the items if one were to purchase them.

The cost is compared with the amount they would have cost the previous year, and hence record how much more expensive living the good life is this year.

94

Create a petition

Ask yourself the following questions:

☐ Is there a hot topic in my industry?
☐ Is there some controversy?
☐ Is something not being done that should be?

If you answered yes to any of these, consider starting a petition about the issue. Thanks to the internet, creating a petition drive is really easy. Sites such as PetitionOnline.com **allow anyone to start a petition for free**. Petitions can and do influence decisions, but whether serious or not, a petition that generates lots of signatures **guarantees great publicity**.

Remember
Journalists understand what you're up to. Don't pretend that your 'Top 10 List' or online petition is earth-shattering, and they'll play along with you and still give you some great media coverage.

9 Internal PR – a neglected essential

The internal audience

Now that jobs for life have virtually disappeared, the need for effective internal communications has never been greater. The struggle for **competitive edge** now demands that staff are more important than they have ever been, for without their

* empathy
* individuality
* flexibility

* creativity
* intuitive thinking
* commitment

there is little to differentiate one business from another. That well-worn phrase 'our staff are our most important asset' has taken on a new meaning.

Employees have **needs and aspirations** that should be met if a company is to succeed. Good communications are essential to this, but there is often an **obvious rift** in many companies between the majority of the workforce and the upper echelons of management.

For too long, companies have ignored internal communications while spending huge amounts on advertising and image raising for external audiences. Think **how much better** it could have been had there been a company-wide culture wherein all employees could have felt free to make **constructive suggestions** for the common good of the firm.

The need for effective internal communications has never been greater

Effective internal communications

In principle, the best-practice communications blueprint will mean that the bulk of general information is available to everybody in the organization with as few exclusions as possible. The real challenges of internal communications are to capture the full creative potential of the workforce through:

* encouraging
* managing
* directing
* harnessing.

Internal communications, whatever their origin, are normally distributed through two specific channels:

* communications department
* human resources.

Both departments must **work hand in hand** for effective internal communications to take place. Employees need to feel that they can **help set the agenda**, allowing problems to be discussed openly and honestly. Only that way can customer service ever really be effective.

Many HR departments communicate too little, and they're only too happy to hand everything over to the communications department.

The quality of a manager's relationship with his team is key to an employee's feelings of well-being, satisfaction and performance. So the more information you can give employees, within reason, the better they're going to feel about it.

'The single biggest problem in communication is the illusion that it has taken place.'
George Bernard Shaw

Employee surveys

An **employee survey** is one way of gauging where to start in this process. A survey can be carried out using an intranet, with emailed answers to a central processing department.

Anonymity is the key here, and your people must be convinced that what they say won't be held against them, or the whole exercise will be a waste of time.

For this reason, it is common to use outside survey firms who can guarantee anonymity and impartiality. Be prepared, though, if you do open the Pandora's box, not only to read the answers, but do something about them as well.

Be prepared not only to read the answers, but also to do something about them

You should ask your people to indicate their level of agreement to a number of statements in a checklist such as:

- ☐ This is a **good company** to work for.
- ☐ I understand the **company's goals** and priorities.
- ☐ The company has a **good reputation**.
- ☐ I am **confident in the future** of the company.
- ☐ Senior management **does a good job** of managing the company overall.
- ☐ My function is **well managed**.
- ☐ I **feel loyal** to the company.

Done properly, this type of survey can produce much useful information, which can have a very positive effect on staff morale.

Towards a communications strategy

A communications strategy needs to reflect a culture in which **values** are of more importance than words in a mission statement.

* A **consistency of communication** across the company is vital if people are to play their full role in any changes that will affect both themselves and the company.
* The plan needs to be sufficiently **detailed** to define what media are to be used throughout the organization, and that the strategy defines the media, rather than vice versa.
* The communication should aim to be a **dialogue** rather than one way, to foster employee engagement.

> If people are expected to do things without proper explanation, they will always blame the messenger rather than the message.

* The real benefits of employee communications result from **getting the listening right**, rather than telling people what's going on from the top of the organization.

After all, it's the **frontline staff** who are often closest to any customer problems. By listening to them, you will have a better-motivated workforce and gain valuable **feedback** from which to create a more honed customer strategy.

A non-confrontational feedback system can give the company the information it needs to improve matters.

Involving staff

When **management** show they **care about their staff**, then people feel more involved with the aims of the company. If they are not involved in the process of change itself, how can they be expected to feel an **involvement** and belief that things are really changing?

Naturally there are times when **confidentiality** demands that delicate information cannot be released early; but in that case the employees should always be told at the same time as the official announcement.

> Verbal communication is just as much about listening as speaking, and it is unfortunate that with many people, listening does not come naturally.

If everyone concentrates on imparting information, who will be left to receive all the messages?

The **principles** of good internal communication can be encapsulated in the following:

1 Consider how you would want to **receive** messages rather than how you would impart them.
2 Think how you might **react** to someone else giving you the particular message you want to give out yourself.
3 Only then, turn the situation on its head and **impart** your message, knowing it will be received in the best possible way.

Remember
Nothing comes close to having a quiet word in someone's ear.

One of the most valuable messages to communicate can be summed up in one simple phrase: **'Thank you!'**

10 Don't turn a crisis into a drama!

Effective crisis communications

None of us likes to think the unthinkable, but every business needs to **plan ahead** to scenarios where crisis management comes into play. It's all too easy for the media to dictate the agenda during a major crisis, and it is therefore the task of senior management to **try to take control in this situation**.

If crisis communications are ignored there is a danger that a serious business disruption will stimulate negative news coverage about the organization. Surviving intense **public scrutiny** with reputation intact will almost certainly not happen unless preparations are made for dealing with a crisis scenario.

Companies face crises all the time. They can include:

* product **recalls**
* plant **closings**
* **tainted** products
* a **crime** committed by an employee
* a **branded** item found at a crime scene
* a company leader making a **poor personal decision**.

The fact that we only hear a few stories of this kind in the news illustrates the power of effective crisis communications.

Only by anticipating the needs of the media can companies hope to get through a crisis relatively unscathed

Working with the media

At most large airports many emergency scenarios are **rehearsed regularly**.

CASE STUDY: Rehearsing at Heathrow

Twice a year, at London's Heathrow, an aircraft is deemed to have crash-landed on one of the runways, and a complete rehearsal of all the emergency services swings into operation. The airport's press office is fully involved and the local 'resident' journalists from the national press are invited to do their utmost to get a fictitious scoop for their respective papers, including 'door-stepping' airport workers and emergency crews.

By co-operating in this way, both press officers and journalists have already built up trust between them and are more likely to co-operate if the unthinkable really does happen.

Bullet Guide: Great PR

The media **has a job to do** in meeting deadlines and filling column inches or airtime. Never answer 'no comment', as this can only lead to **speculation on their part,** and you will have a bigger job to try to **kill off rumours** that spread like wildfire.

Journalists will understand if you tell them you need time to check out the facts. But if you tell a journalist that you will get back to him, ensure you do so in a timely manner, even if it is only to say you need more time.

Not knowing what is going on is the one thing calculated to increase media speculation.

'It is generally much more shameful to lose a good reputation than never to have acquired it.'
Pliny The Elder

Advance preparation

Although it is not possible to anticipate every possible crisis within a business, there are some things that **can be done in advance** to **minimize the problems** at a time of crisis:

* **Create a contact sheet**
  The contact sheet should list all the telephone numbers and addresses of the executive board, senior management and key individuals out of hours so that they can be contacted at short notice.
* **Train the key players in media interview techniques**
  There is nothing worse than a company spokesman looking uncomfortable and afraid of being interviewed.

114

* **Plan a room as a media centre**
  It should have **telephone lines** for journalists as well as **internet** access. They will appreciate having such facilities, which make their life easier, and your business will be less inconvenienced by them in the long term.

Some crises are **not always recognized for what they are** until almost after the event. Some companies unwittingly **turn a drama into a crisis** purely through lack of communication; others have a crisis plan in place and run it as if they are on autopilot to great effect.

A leader who has a strong grasp of the issues and can communicate effectively with reporters is essential. A CEO who lacks media skills should be trained properly or kept out of high-profile media encounters.

Creating a crisis plan

Consider a crisis plan an **insurance policy** for your corporate image. If a crisis hits, you can spend **crucial time** implementing the plan rather than trying to figure out where to start.

Preparedness can include:

* developing a detailed crisis strategy
* creating media materials in advance
* arranging media training for key executives
* pre-establishing a crisis team.

When a crisis hits

1 Gather as much information about the situation as quickly as possible and from a variety of sources.
2 Talk with your legal counsel and your communications counsel to see what information can be released and what should remain confidential.

3 Stay in constant contact with your senior management or crisis team.
4 If any lives are in jeopardy, make sure you **immediately address** those concerns.
5 Be sure that any information you release to the media or the public is **truthful**. If something you say is false, your **credibility will be irreparably damaged**.
6 Do your best to **understand** what the public's concerns will be, and **address** those concerns directly.
7 Make sure your own employees and clients are **never surprised by information going out** to the public. Leaks to the media from your own staff or important stakeholders make great fodder for negative media stories.

The press interview itself should never be the first time you hear the tough questions

Remember

The cardinal rule of media relations – never more so than at times of crisis – is to **be prepared**.

* In most cases you won't have advance warning of a crisis, so it's crucial that your staff have already carried out simulations of possible scenarios.
* Role play before every media encounter.

Be **sympathetic** to those affected by the issue at hand. Never overlook the power of **common sense** in your handling of a crisis.

Every organization has blind spots that can lead to embarrassing media gaffes, so make sure you:

* study previous media clips
* read what the press are saying about you
* develop a media relations strategy to mend fences or create new opportunities.

While no one can predict a crisis, **appropriate foresight** can mean the difference between maintaining an excellent corporate reputation and the dreadful alternative.

What next?

By its very nature, this book can only skim the surface of what can be a daunting subject. Books that go into more detail include the following:

Brown, Rob, *Public Relations and the Social Web: How to Use Social Media and Web 2.0 in Communications* (London: Kogan Page, 2009)

Gardner, Paula, *Do Your Own PR: The A-Z of Growing Your Business Through The Press, Networking & Social Media* (Great Yarmouth: Lean Marketing Press, 2009)

Green, Andy, *Creativity in Public Relations (PR In Practice)* (London: Kogan Page, 2001)

Gregory, Anne, *Planning and Managing Public Relations Campaigns: A Strategic Approach: A Step-by-step Guide (PR In Practice)* (London: Kogan Page, 2000)

Kirshenbaum, Richard, Yaverbaum, Eric, Bly, Robert W. and Benun, Ilise, *Public Relations For Dummies* (Indianapolis: John Wiley, 2006)

Langford-Wood, Naomi, and Salter, Brian, *Critical Corporate Communications: A Best Practice Blueprint (CBI Fast Track)* (Chichester: John Wiley, 2002)

Phillips, David and Young, Philip, *Online Public Relations: A Practical Guide to Developing an Online Strategy in the World of Social Media (PR In Practice)* (London: Kogan Page, 2009)

Scott, David Meerman, *The New Rules of Marketing and PR: How to Use Social Media, Blogs, News Releases, Online Video, and Viral Marketing to Reach Buyers Directly* (Hoboken: John Wiley, 2010)

Theaker, Alison, *The Public Relations Handbook (Media Practice)* (London: Routledge, 2011)